Roger Mortimer

THE HUMAN RACE COULD NEVER MAKE A SINGLE SOUL

"Each one shall find again his dismal tomb, Shall reassume his flesh
and his own figure, Shall hear what through eternity re-echoes."

So we passed onward o'er the fitly mixture Of shadows and rain with
footsteps slow, Touching a little on the future life.

INFERNO CANTO VI - X

The Divine Comedy by Dante Alighieri, translated by Henry Longfellow.

Thanks to Margreta Chance for her help with editing this book.

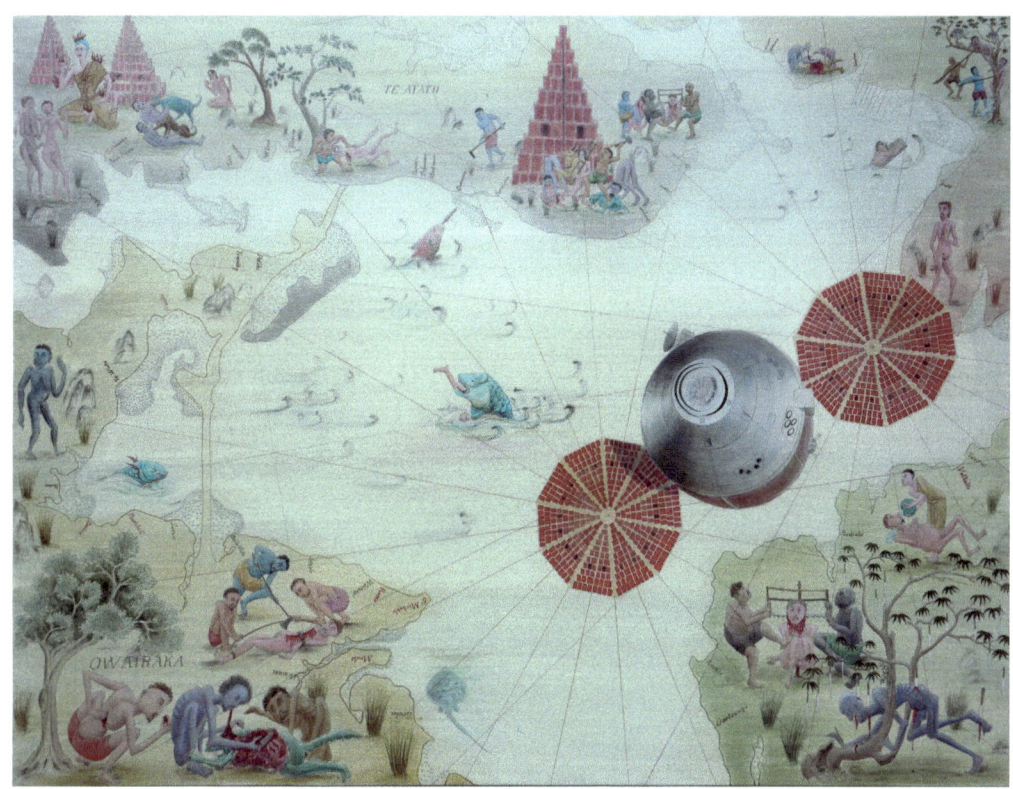

Roger Mortimer 1956-
Saint Michael 2013
Ink and acrylic lacquer on canvas 1220 x 910mm

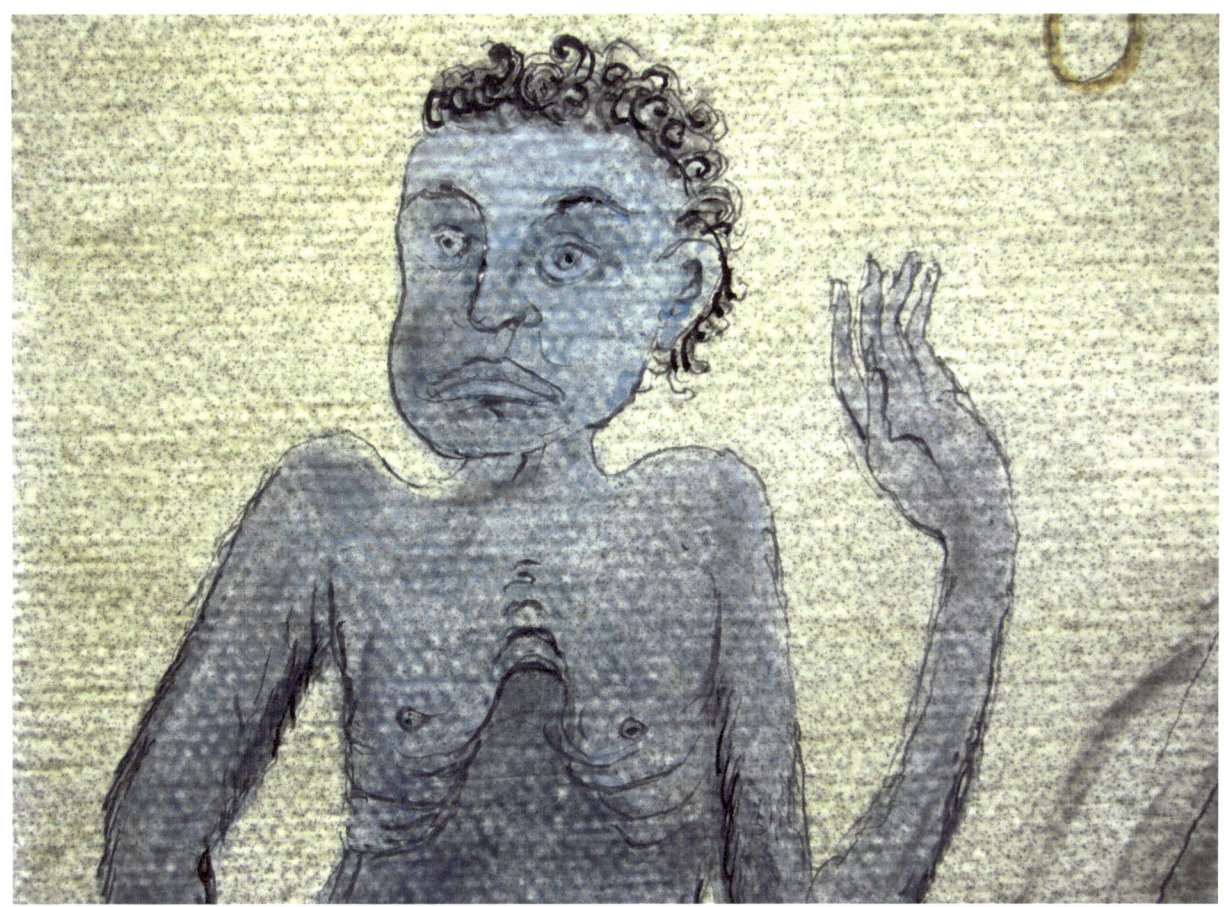

Each one shall find in his business, a flash and a stone figure.

The showers here in town echo a filthy mixture of rain and shadow, like footsteps slowly catching on the future.

What torments here?

Will they listen to me burning?

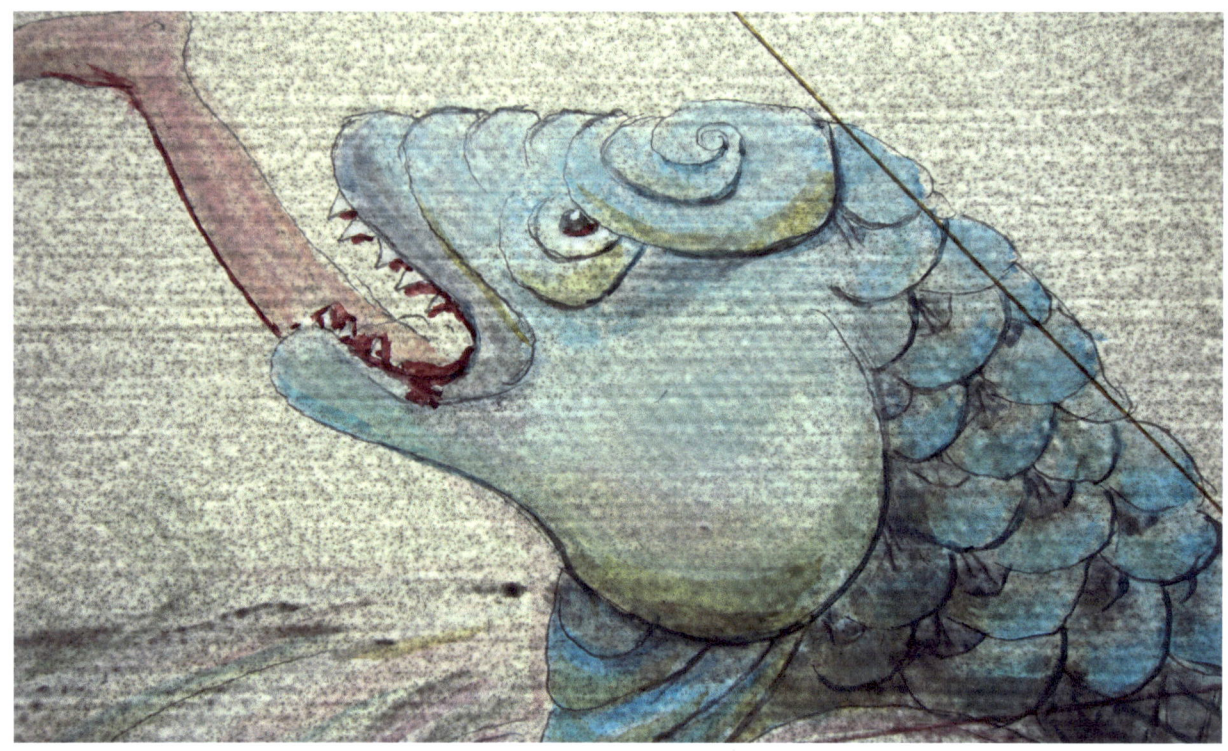

These people, maladaptive to true perfection, never contain more than they look to be.

Round in a circle we went speaking.

We came to a point in the street where we found our great enemy.

That fucking voice. That commitment. That sage who encouraged me.

He said, "Let right by fear and power, and via for your own rage."

He may have shown up to prevent us going down a crag.

This is this journey to the office.

This is a world on the highway, when Michael wrought vengeance upon the proud.

Even the sales women could be sent to earth by this cruel monster.

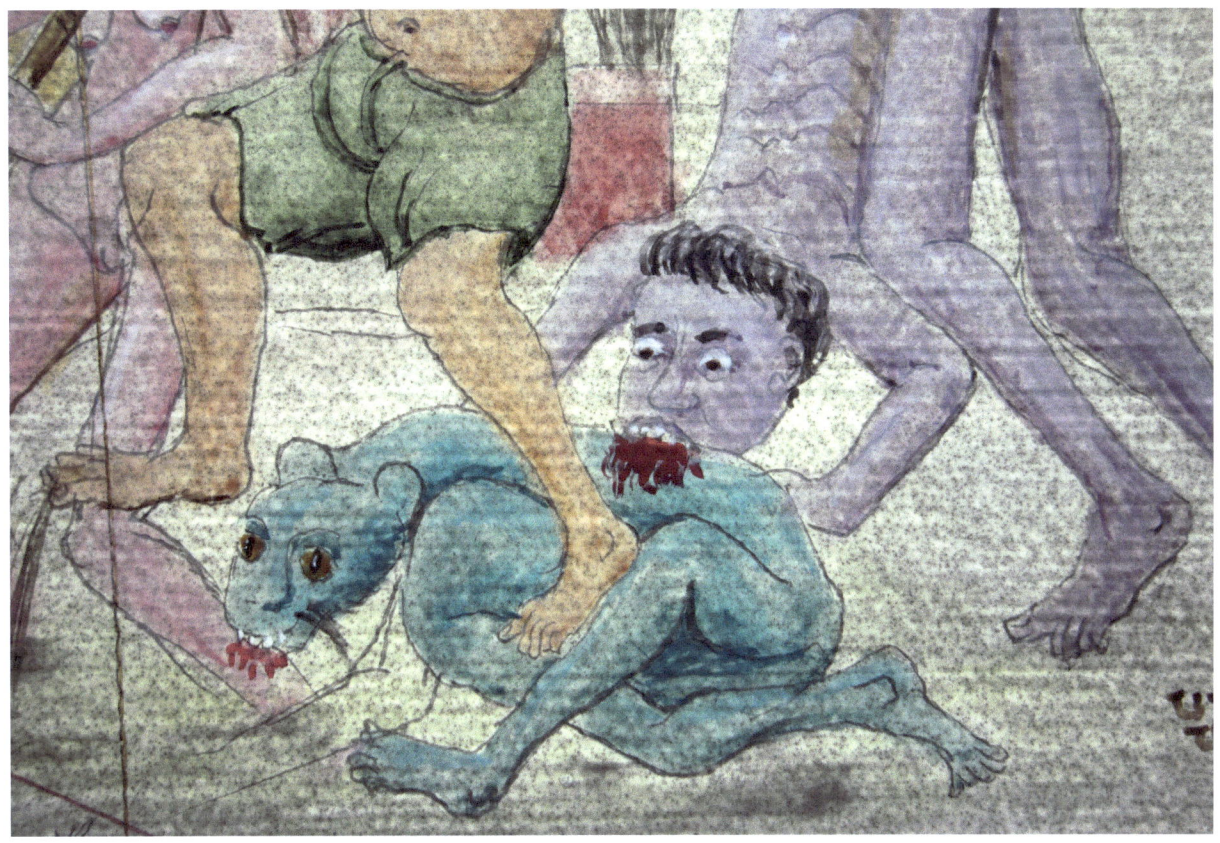

Send Him rustling forth into the chasm, this Sex God who heaps on new toils and sufferings.

I wiped off, without transgression, much waste while He danced a roundelay.

I saw people, more than elsewhere, forced to roll weights forward.

With great howls they clashed together, and they pointed to each other crying,

"Why? Why keepers and squanderers?"

(In a bus, we returned along the little road pointing and shouting.)

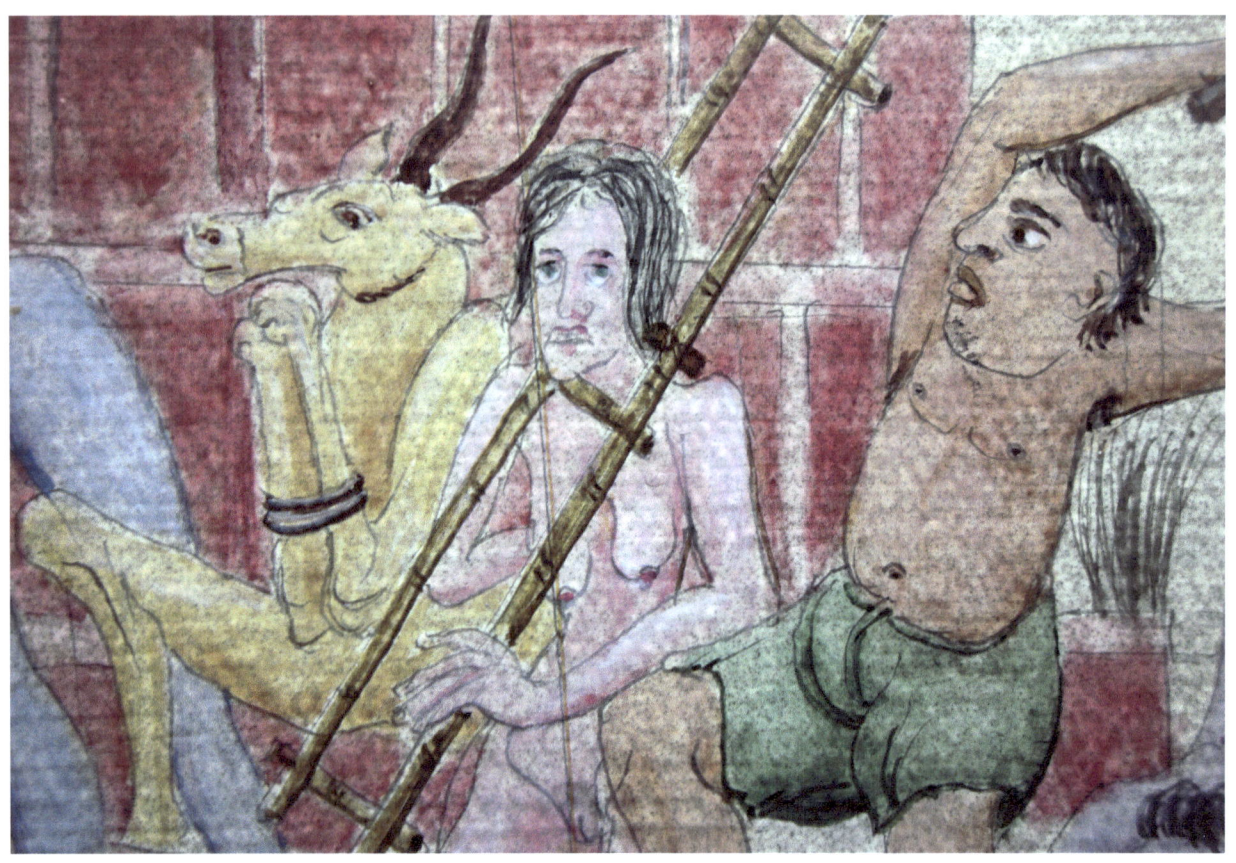

Each one here wheels about turning half circle to another journalist.

How clear it is to me what people are. All clerics wearing shaven crowns.
All of them squirt first life, and so they measure and know spending.

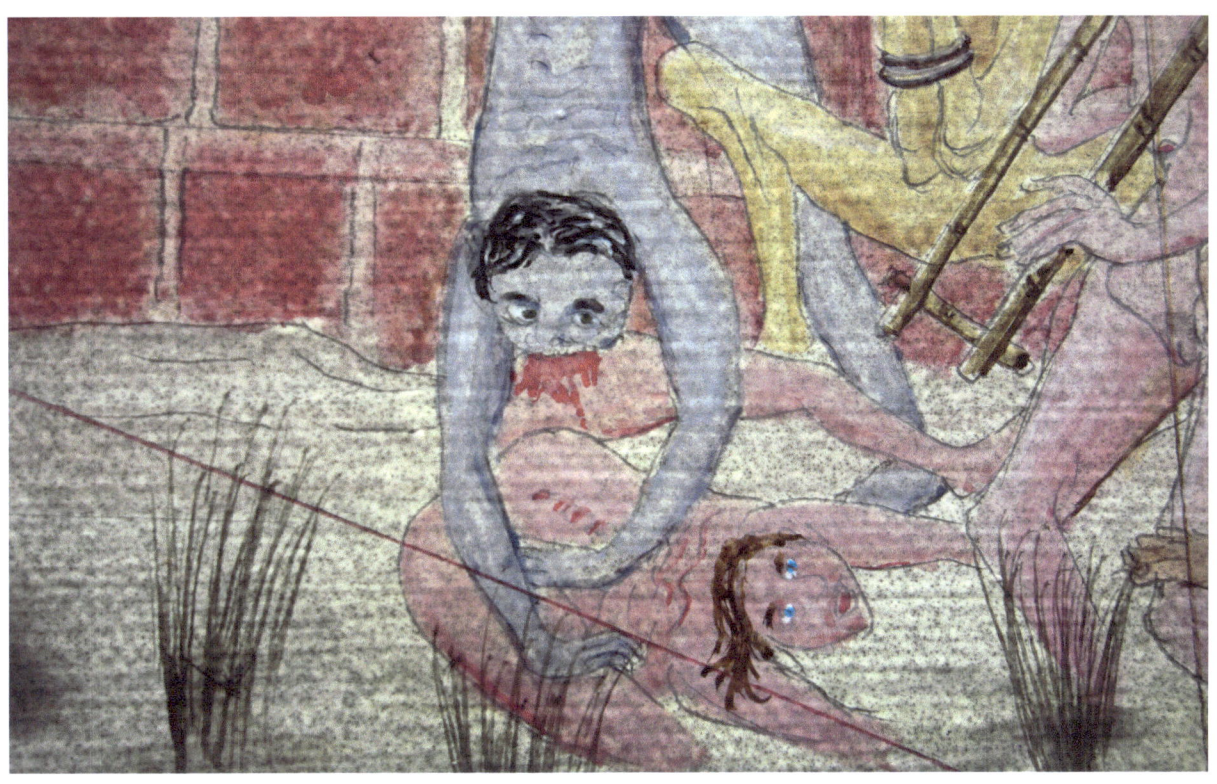

Know the hairy covering that cloaks the head of all hopes.

Idle forces recognise some of us, who are affected by His melodies.

I hate the thought that I'll entertain creating lists, concerning life.

And I can't stand transient fast goods. Worse, I can't stand there being no words.

(Forever shall I come and buy things from the Super Car.)

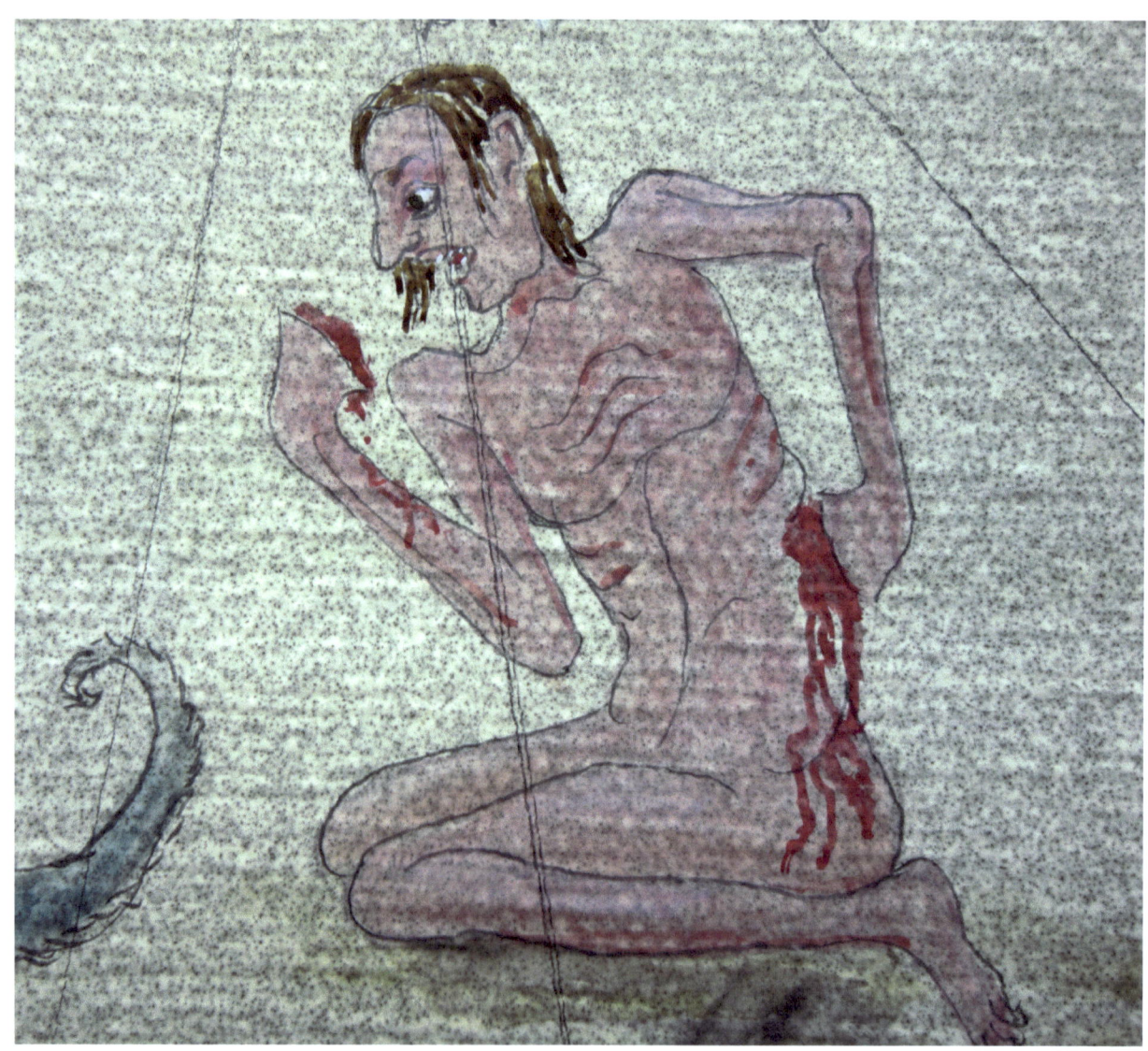

What is this fortune? What has the world so within its clutches? What I have learnt?

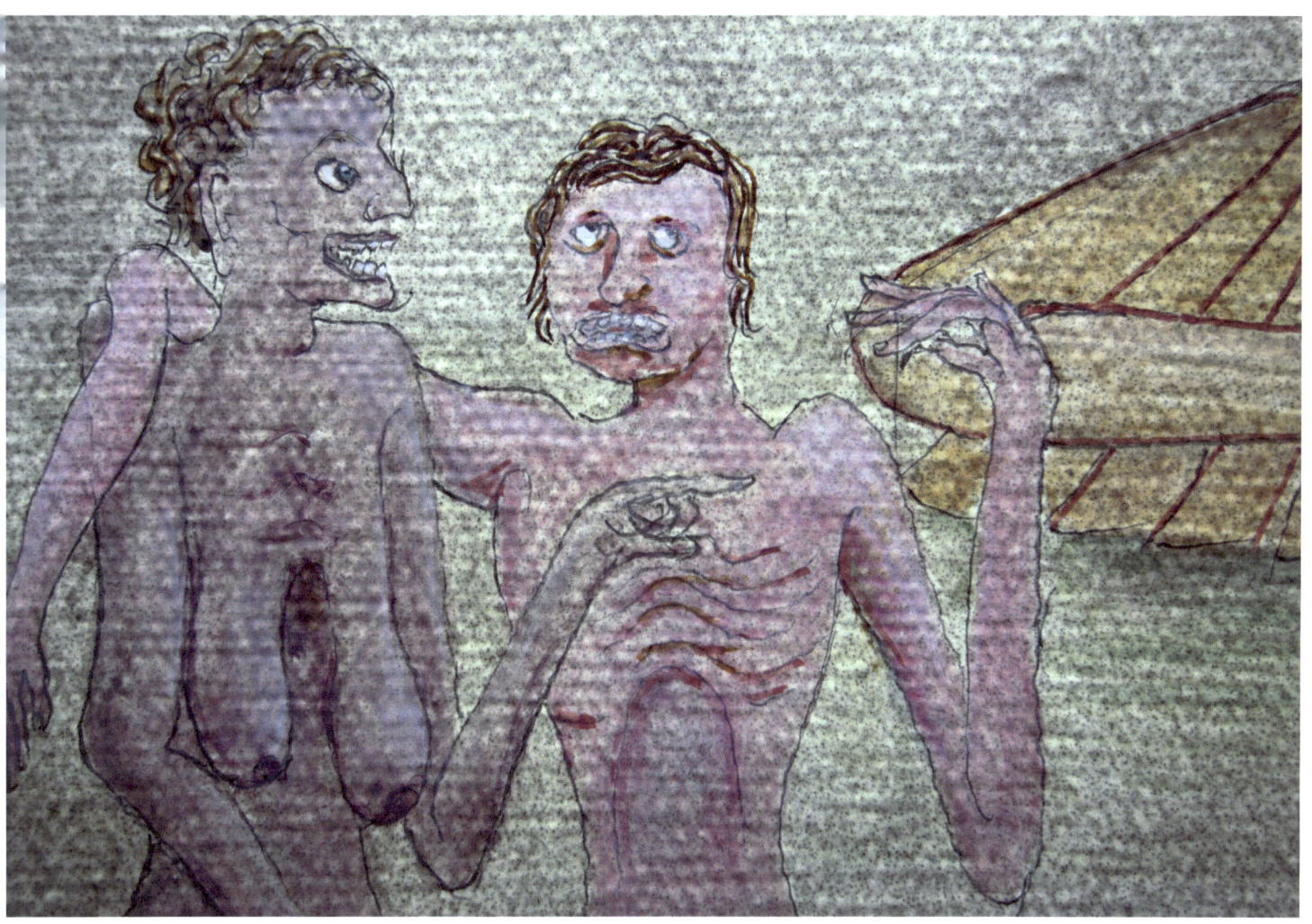

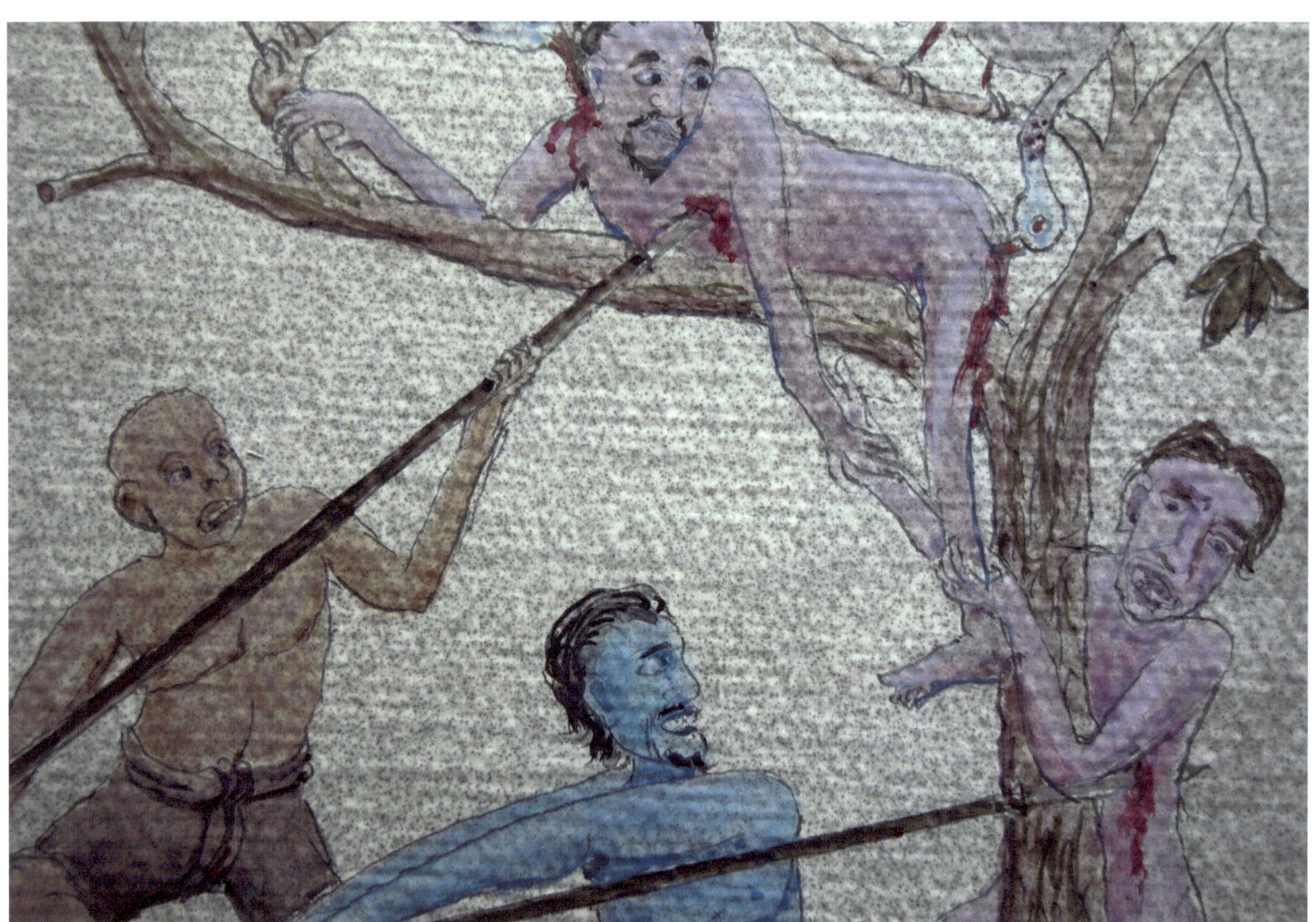

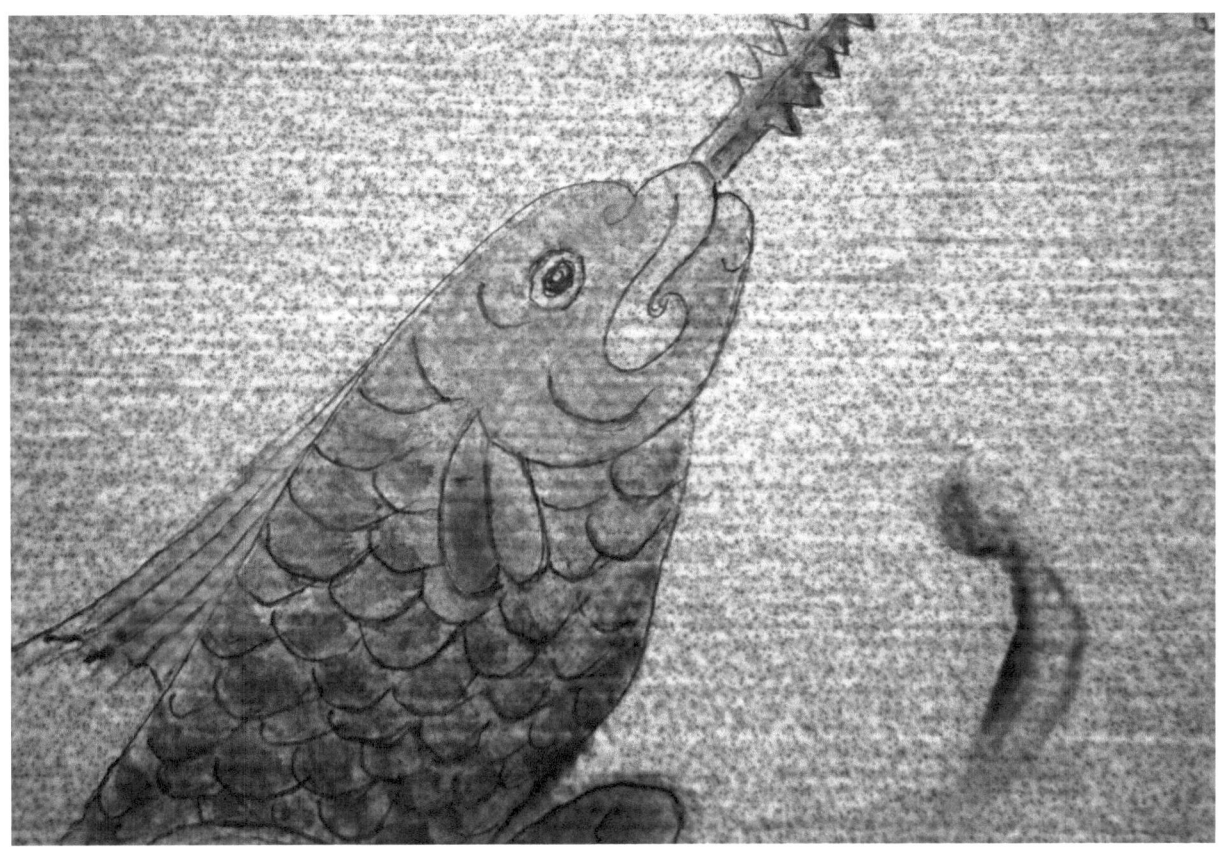

He rides on a seal.

Everything transcends the heavens, distributing light in equal measure.

The mundane splendours gain a general mystery, and change the progress of all human wisdom.

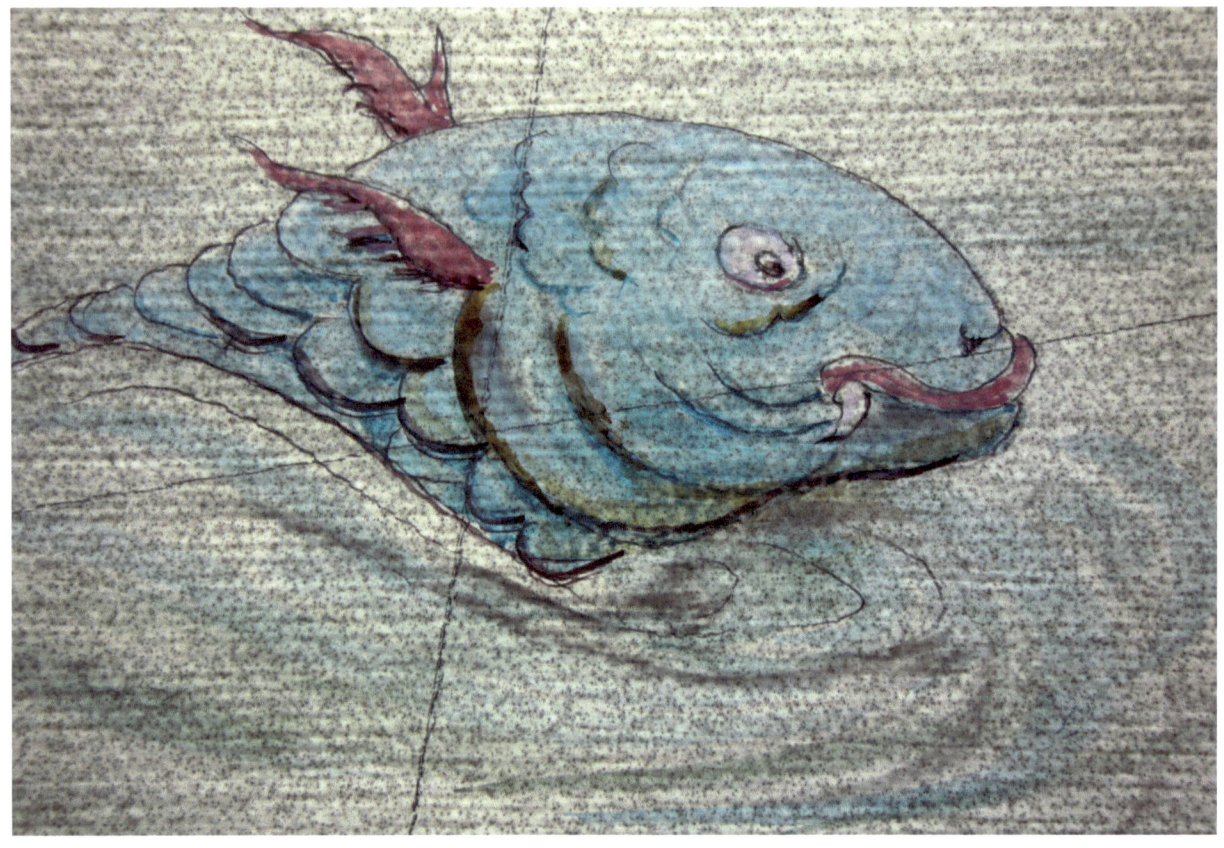

She, this big fish, is crucified by those who get her praise, giving her a blindness.

She is blissful and She hears not other problems.
She rejoices as creatures take turns to decide what and when to monitor the video.

Across on the other bank the water boils itself, and runs out along the gallery.
This water is sombre, and the creature's progress is slow among the dusty waves.

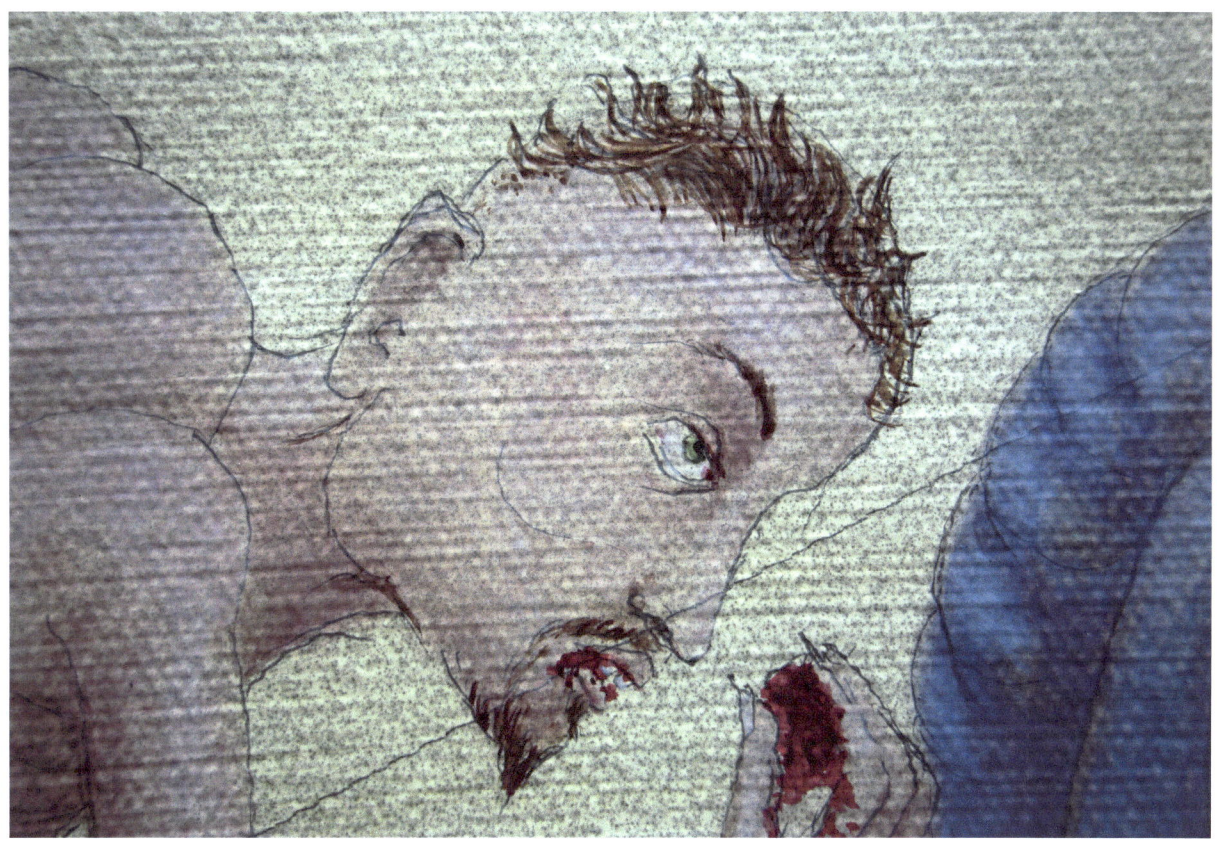

I sit down at the foot of the river bank in grey shorts.

I still intend to hold to these people so that they might look ahead, instead of tearing at each other piecemeal and effective.

Believe the water people.

Make this water turn.

Work this week in the sun, glad that only the sounds are sluggish.

Gurgle in your throats unbroken words we cannot say.

Go around filthy, between the dry bank and the swamp, with eyes turned on those at the foot of the tower.

Before the high tower our eyes looked upward toward the summit.

A scene of discernment.

"What is this fire and who are they that make it?" I thought to myself.

And across the tip of the waves, I beheld a very little boat.

"Come towards us and guide us," I shouted out.

"Hear that Christ, my lord – you're not a stronger person."

He who listens has been done and as such becomes less scared.

Soon the crowd went on its way, diving into the water beneath the surface.

I was running through the gate and in front of me I greeted one who was calloused.

"Isaac! Hello. Are you okay? No work at school today?" I inquired.

My spirit remained sleeping, rather than being defiled.

Then Isaac stretched out both hands saying, "Away dogs to the Lilly Fields."

With his arms clasped around my neck he kissed my face and said,

"With this table so blessed you should be furious with the World Congress."

(I am leaving behind this one horrible kiss.)

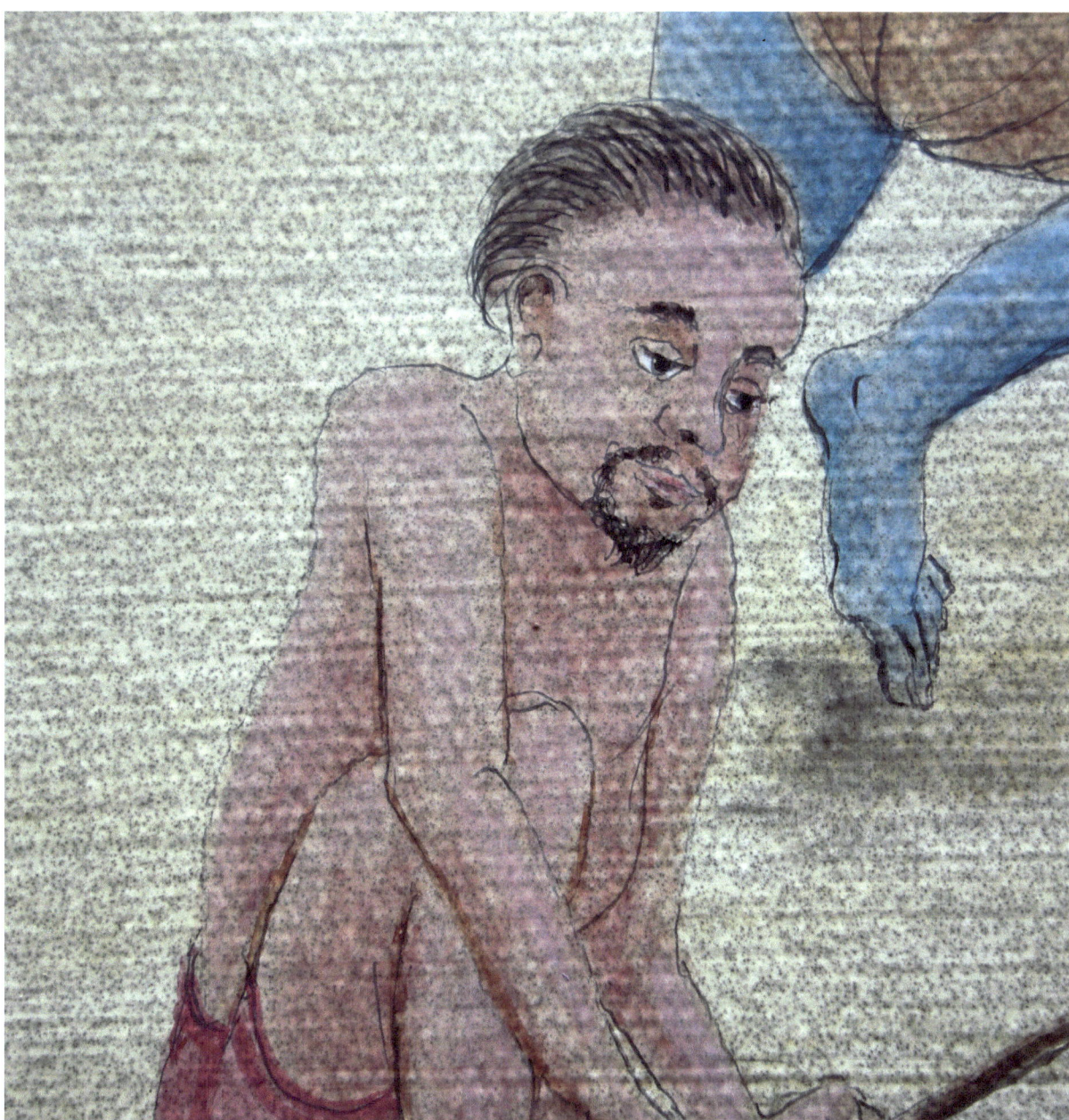

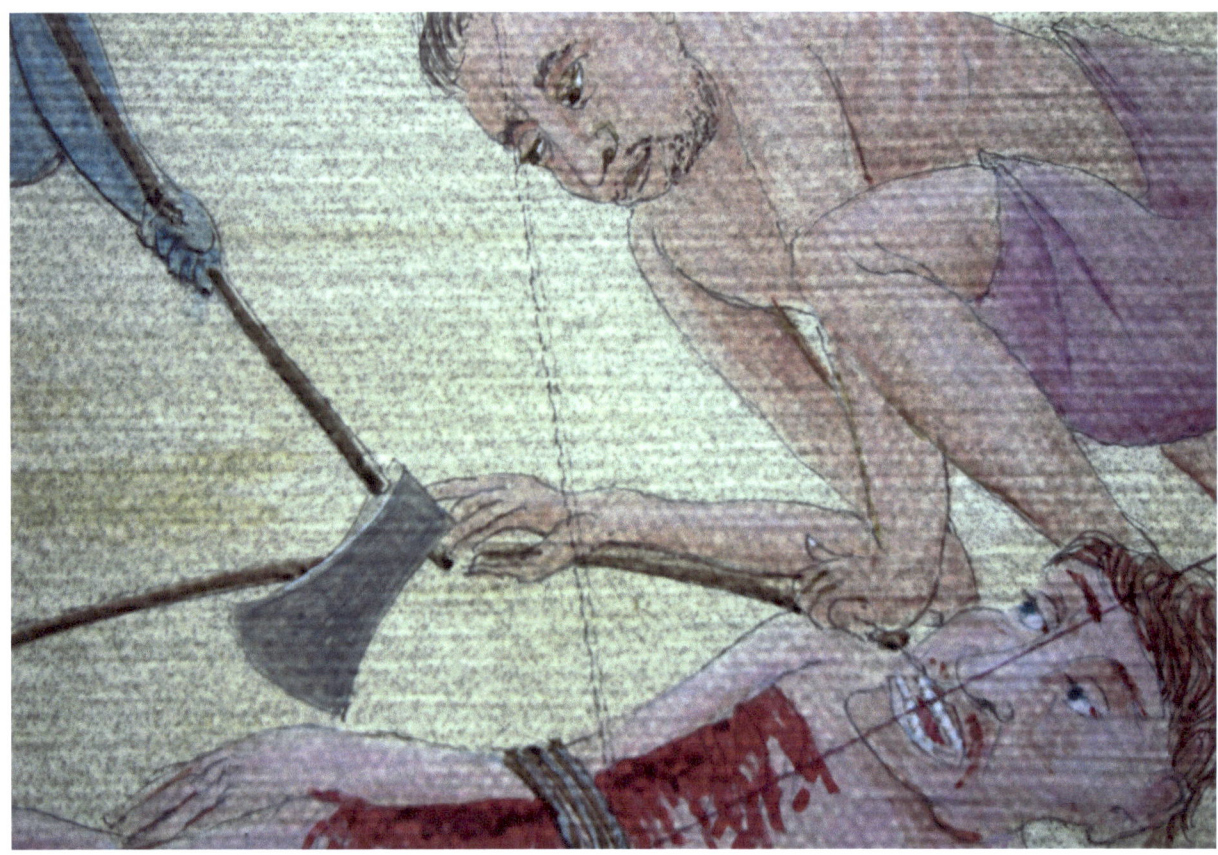

I should be pleased if I could see the spray before we get out of the lake.

A little after, I made my praise to God.

People were all shouting hopefully, "Excess rights guaranteed!"

We left there that night, but my own ears smoked and I barred my eyes.

Even now as the city draws near I ask myself, "What great citizen lies in the wrong grave?

What vermilion hell lies there in that valley?"

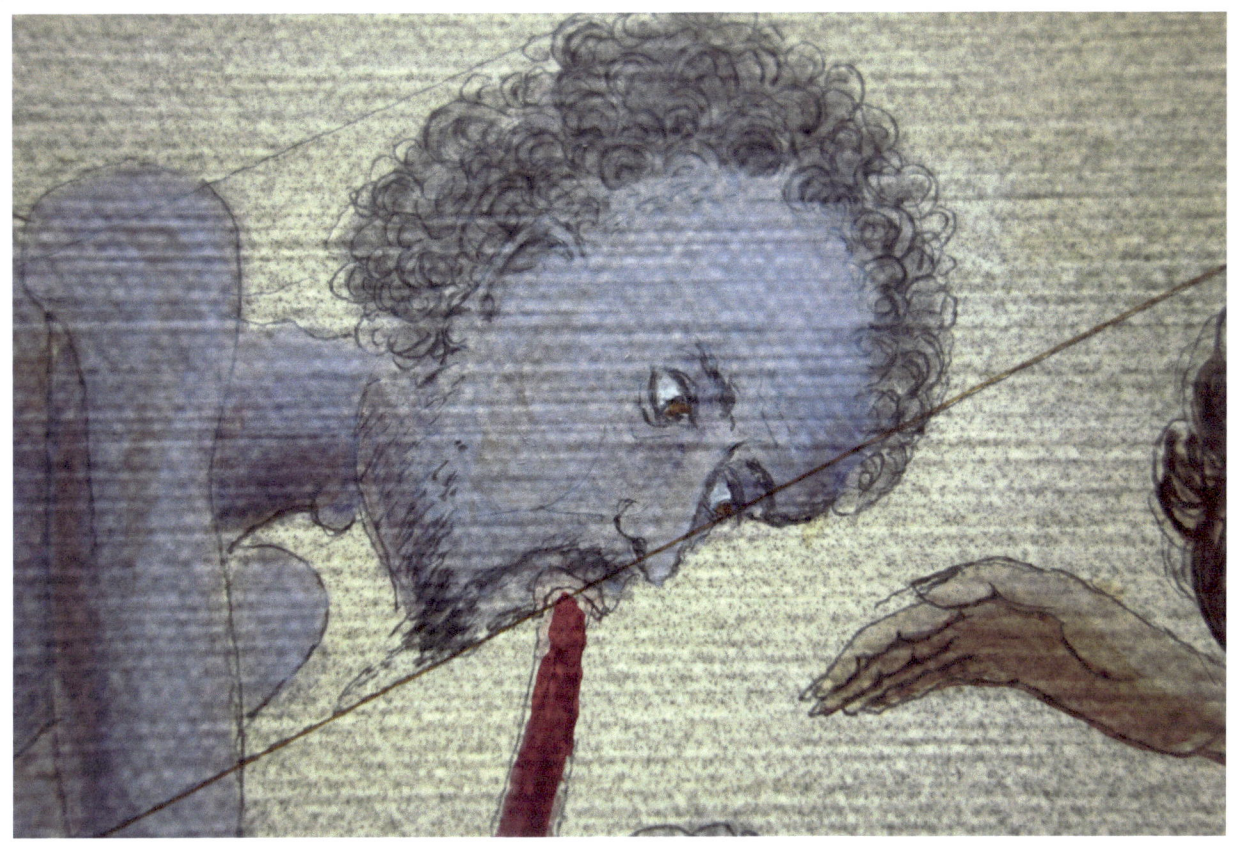

We held a profound discussion at the walls of the city.

We then came to a place where loud parties were crying out to us.

More than one thousand at the gate angrily chanting, "Who is this out there? Who is this out there?"

A kingdom of these people made their song, and they called this great day Vallone.

(Begone anybody who enters these dominions.)

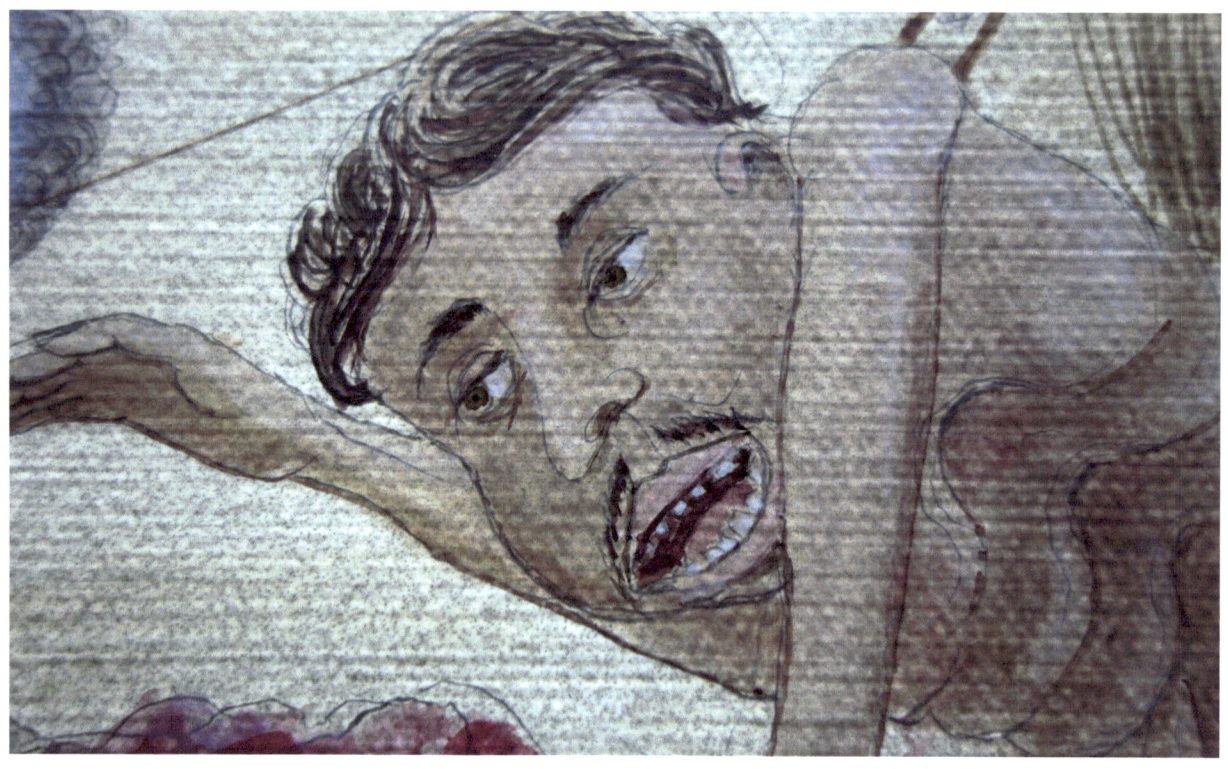

I returned alone along the road made for school research.

I was discomforted, my first thoughts were, "Never return here."

Oh my dear, seven times I have been rendered secure and drawn from peril.

I do not deserve to be sick and to be denied reprocessed lettuce.

(Lord I fear not moments of progress.)

Today I wear a spirit that comforts and nourishes me, for in this netherworld I will not leave.

So steadfast I remain, yes and no in my head content.

The crowd closed the portals, and I remained without tension in me.

My eyes were cast down, and my forehead all boldness.

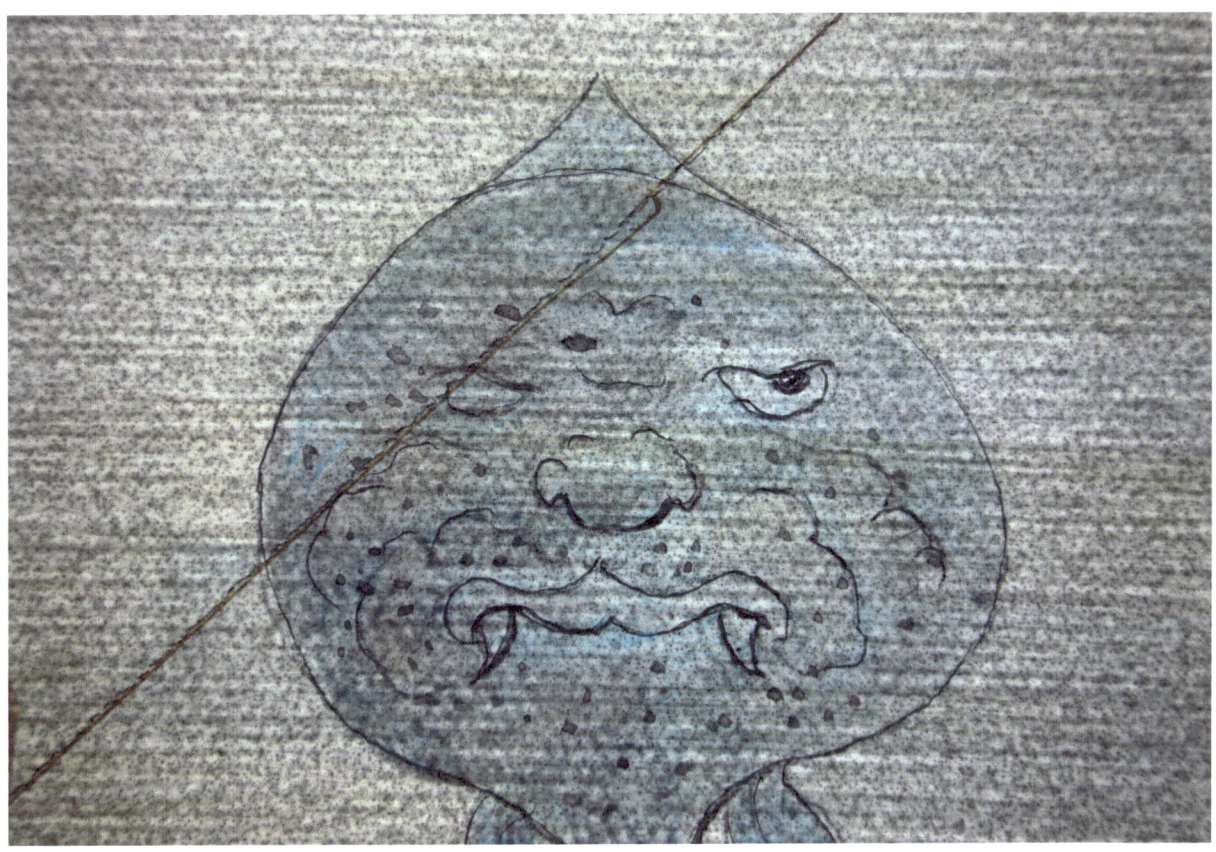

I will conquer these trials, whatever defense this pain is.

The arrogance means nothing once we use the secret code.

The inscription seems to pass across a circle, and by this means the city shall be opened.

I perceived that the words used were quite different from the first time.

This made me fearful because they were written out of broken phrases.

As in the movie *To the Bottom of the Doleful Conch*.

(The scene from which Spain has been cut)

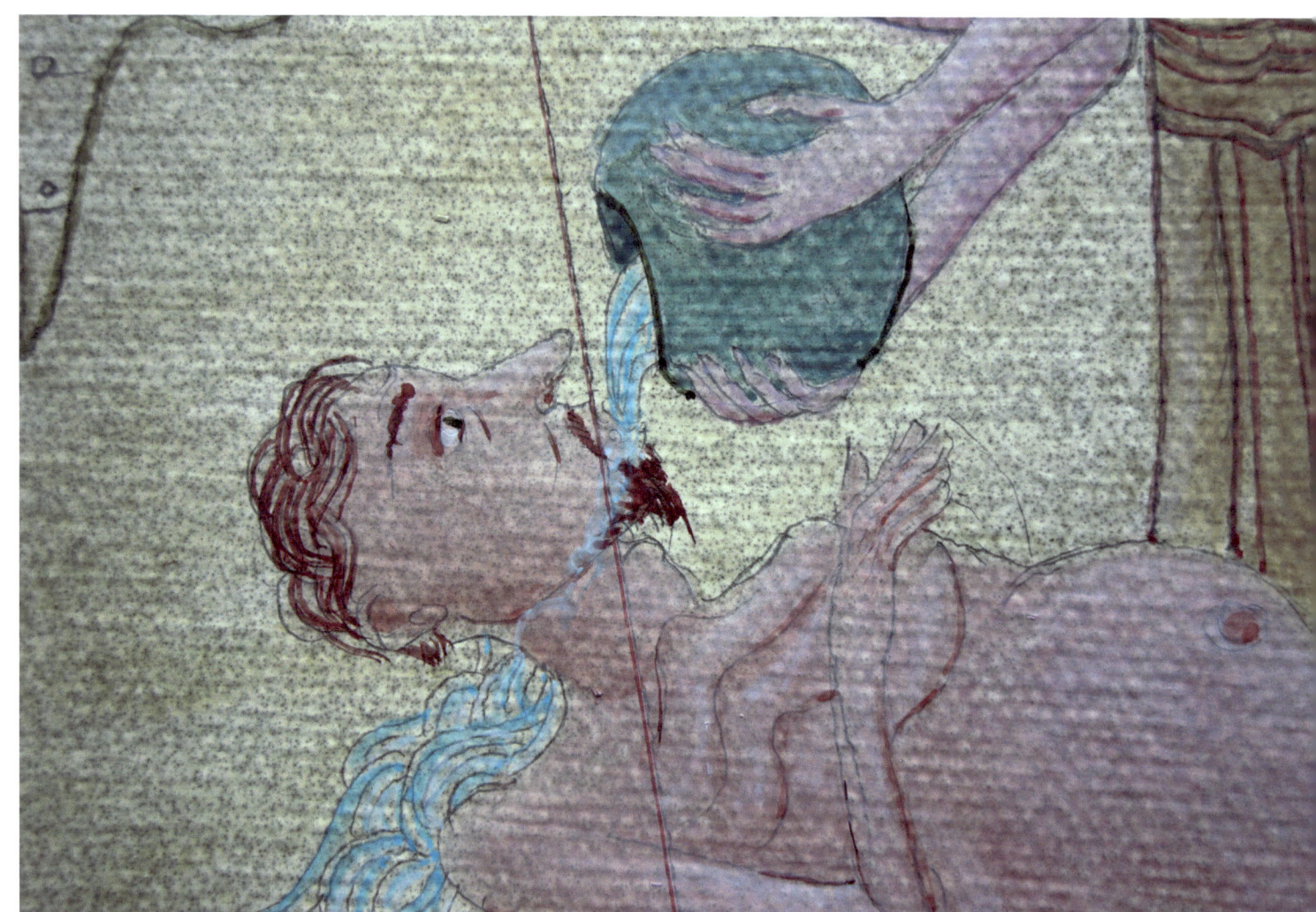

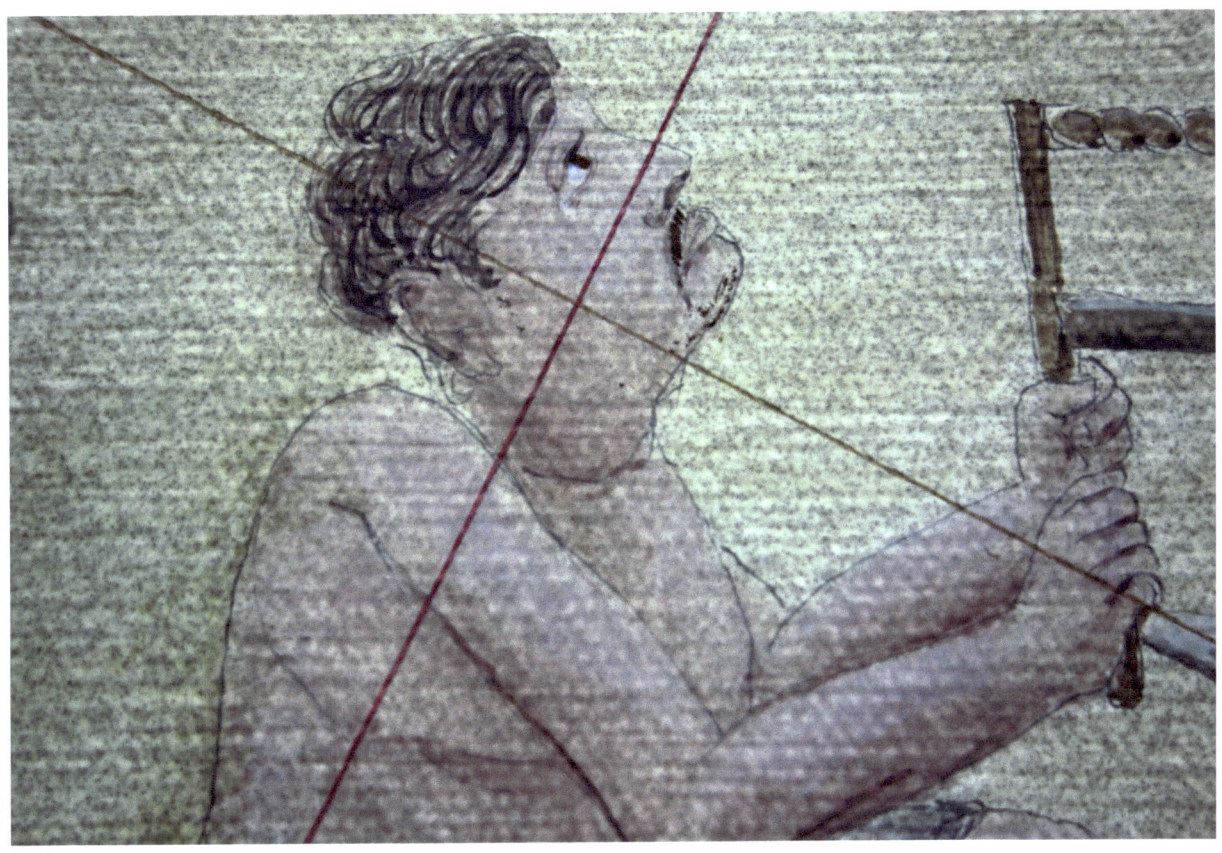

The lowest region, and the darkest, is furthest from the Heaven.

The film, which is pretty, is encompassed by the Dollar.

It shows, once again, that glass was conjured onto the bodies.

By this means the makers brought flesh to the spirit of Jesus.

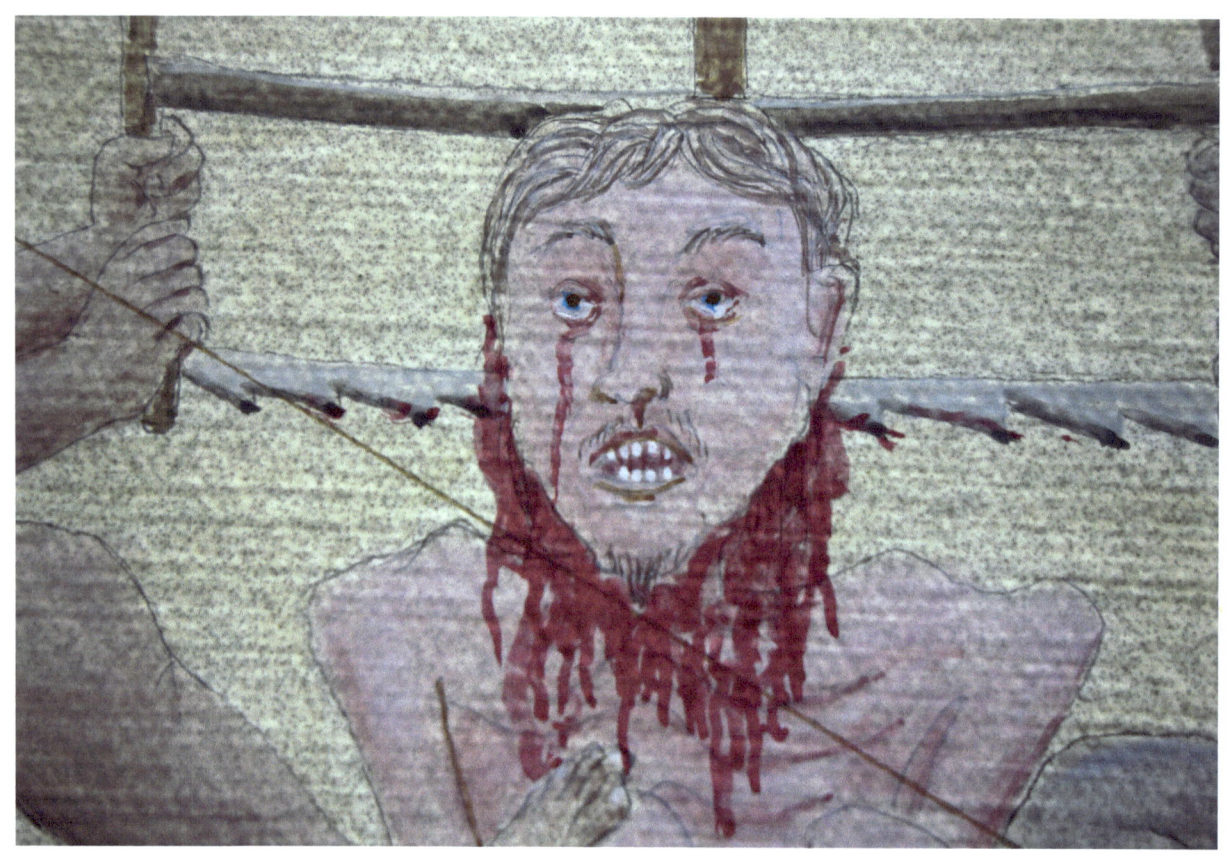

My eyes draw me towards the Hightower with its red flaming summit.

In that moment I saw three women stained with blood, and the greenest goat, small and horrid.

These handmaidens of the Queen of Everlasting Lamentation said to me, "Behold the fierce parents."

On the left-hand side one was weeping, on the right another beat her breast with her palms, crying into her iPhone,

"Stone will change. Evil at our age, we know, is as fierce as the sun."

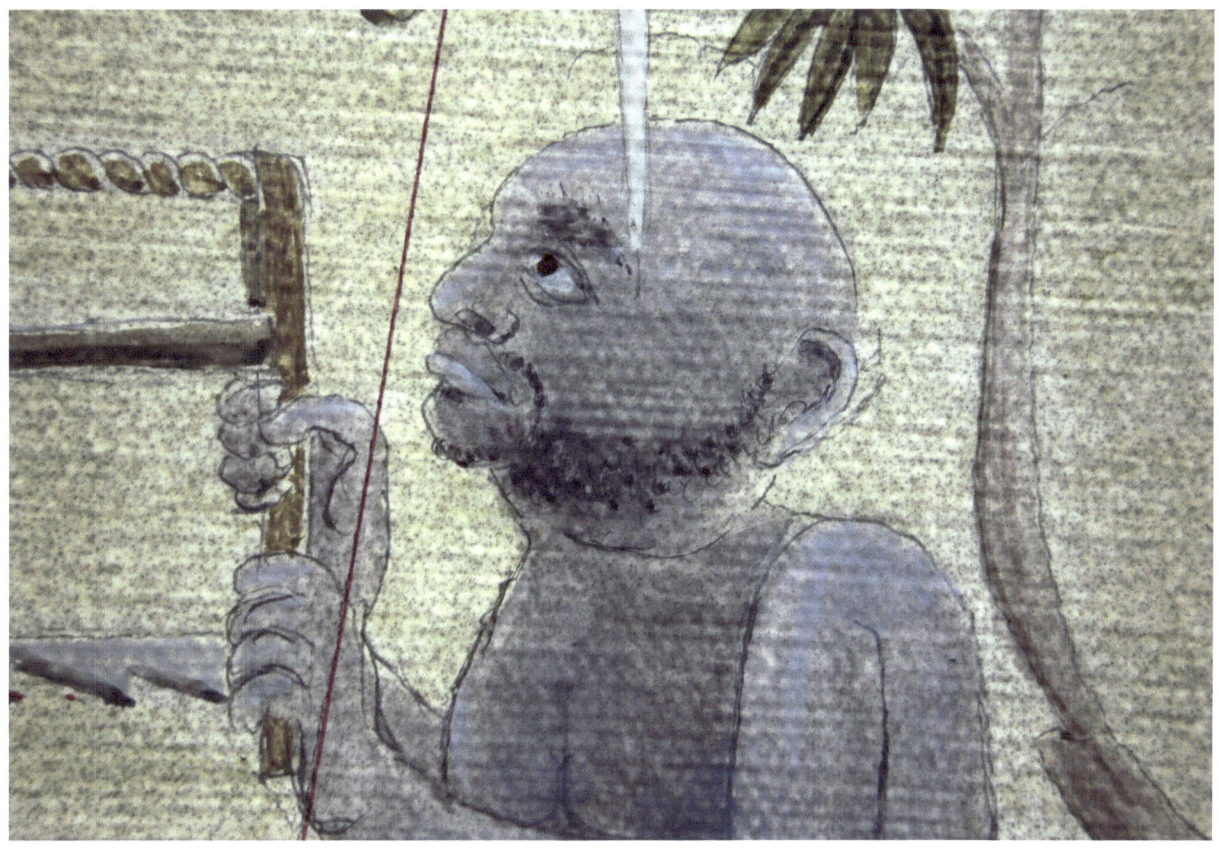

I shall receive no more mothers turning up with their babies.

The three handmaidens turned ugly, and showing interest in my hands they said to me,

"Do you understand that it will take a doctrine to conceal itself beneath the veil of this mysterious verse."

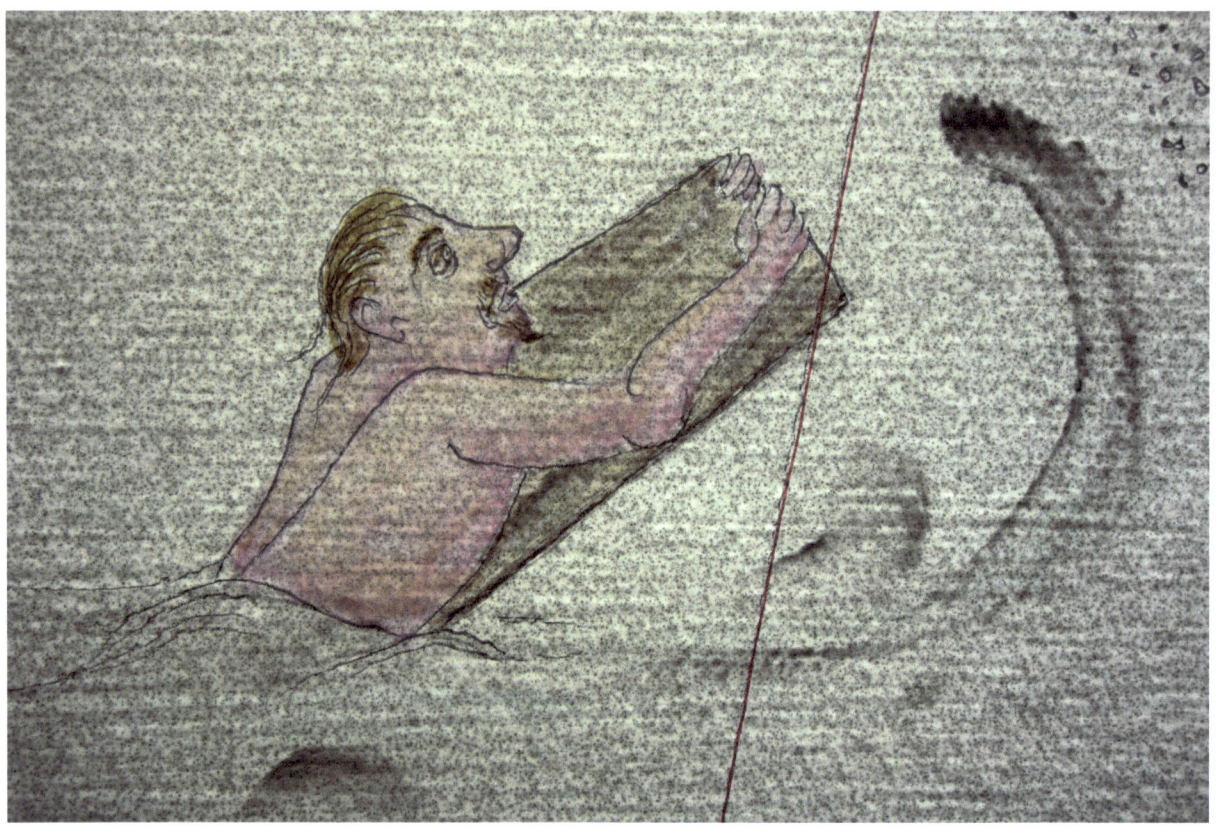

Again He came, across the turbid waves playing God, and both the margins trembled.

The impetuous wind smites, the forest without restraint, and the branches beat down.
Dust goes there, and the wild beasts and their shepherds take flight.

Mine eyes were directed towards a vision of the moon, where the smoke was most intense.
I saw hostile frogs across the water, each one was huddled near.
I saw more than one thousand souls flee from Him, who on foot was passing out the wet steaks.
I saw his office. He was waving his left hand, and only with anguish did He seem to weary.

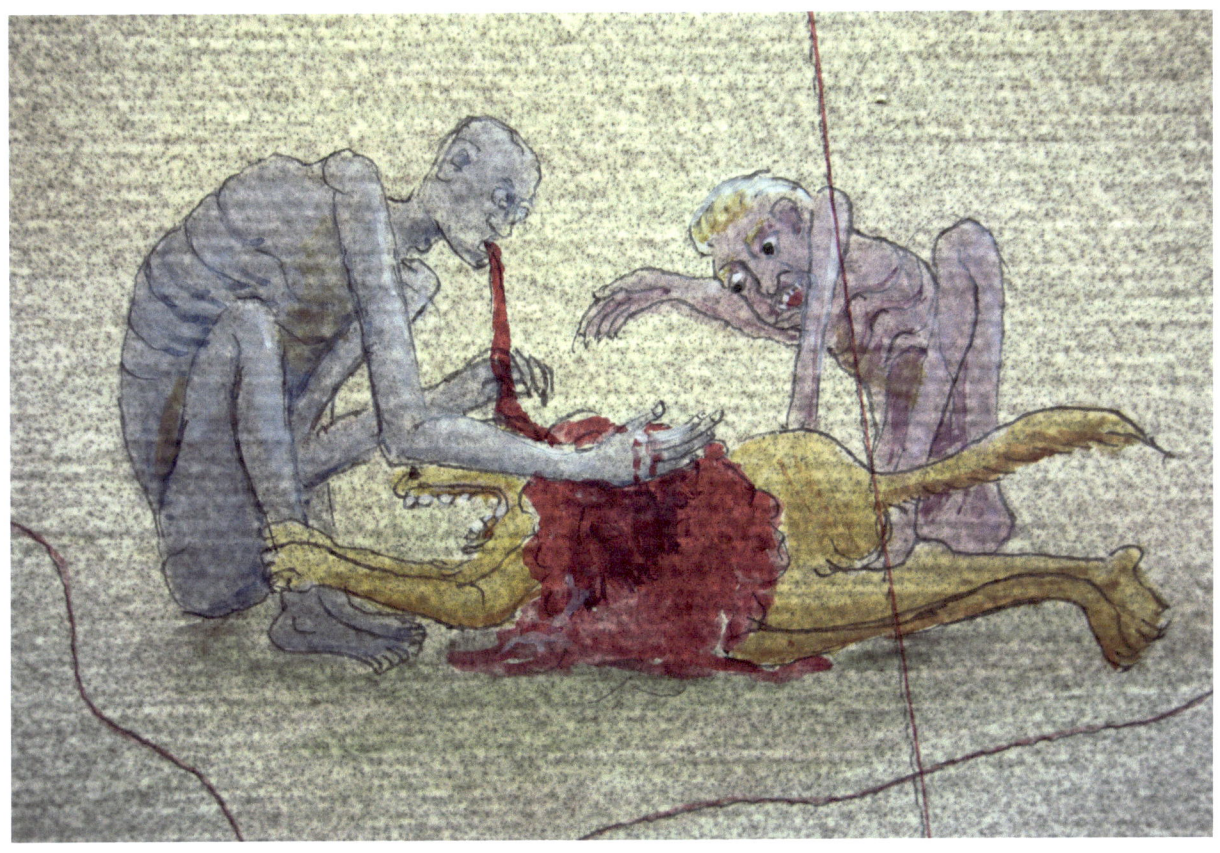

Reach the gate and ride the pussy a little. There is no resistance.

I perceived one sent from heaven.

She said to me, "You may stand quite still and bow. I've banished out of heaven those people who despise the threshold.

Those recalcitrant against that world, from which the end can never be."

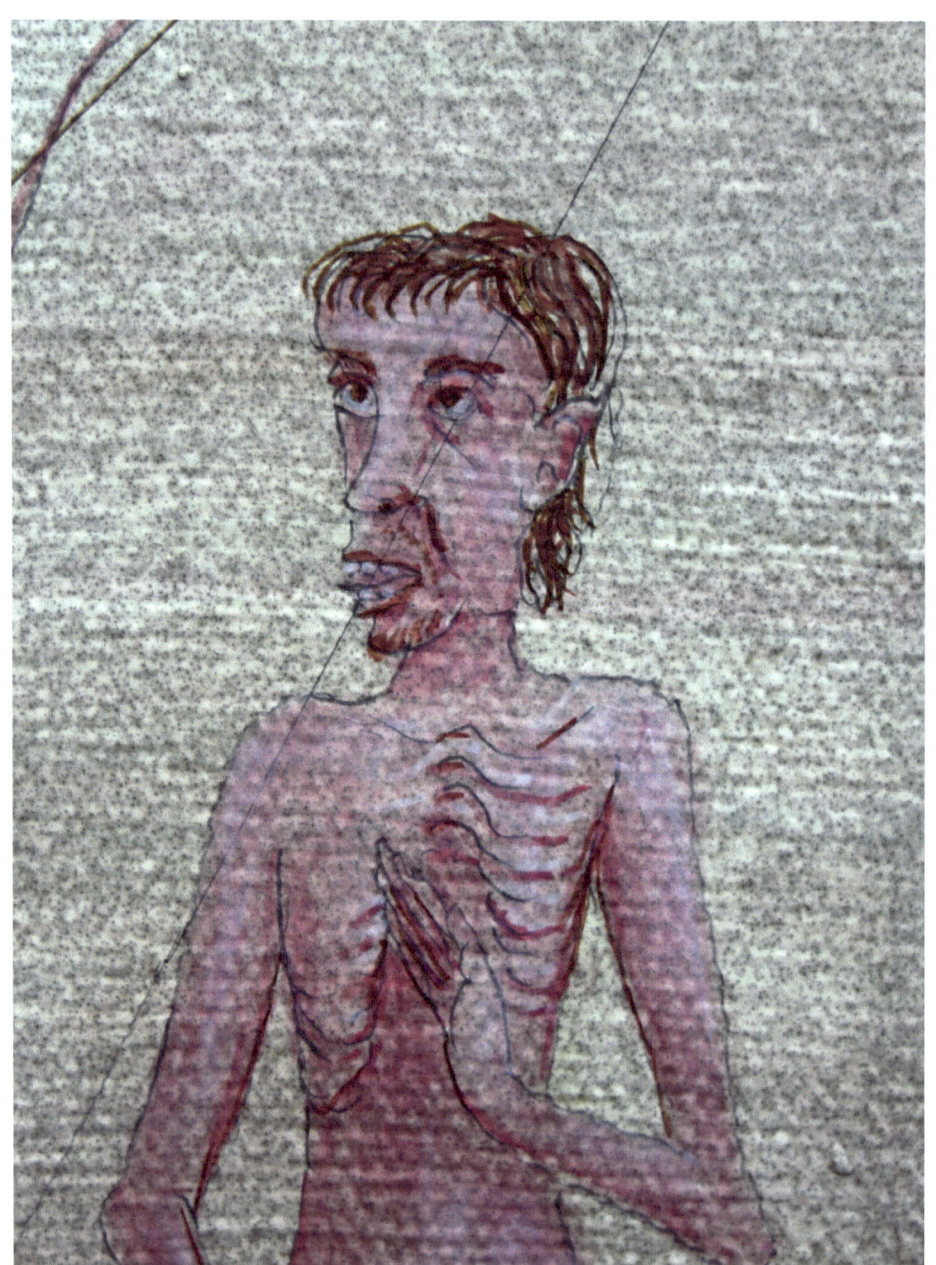

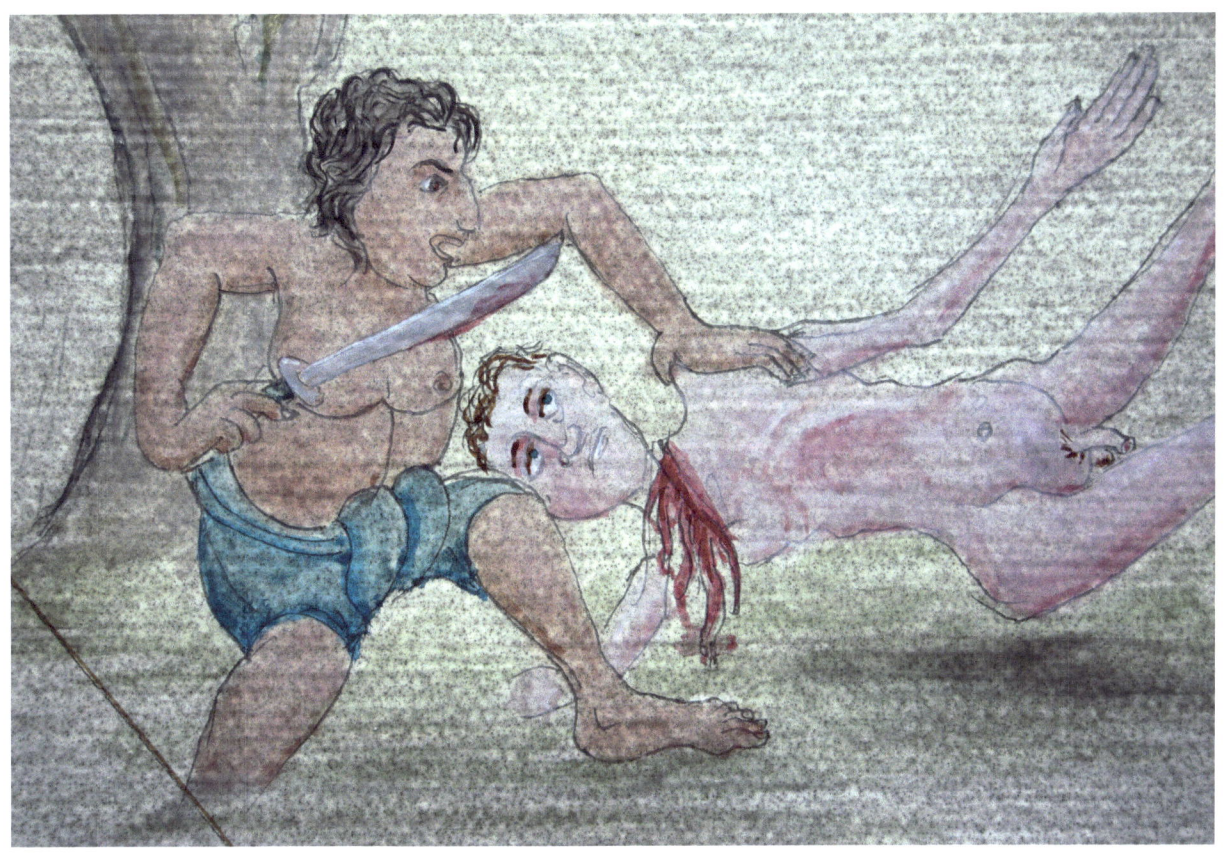

"Can you return along the road and walk with me?" She asked.

"I have to look at another care constraint before we go," She continued.

"I find the present status directed towards the city, unholy.

Every hand will pay for this terrible torment, as the arts grow stagnant."

(We entered without any context, and I hated to see in what condition such a fortress was held.)

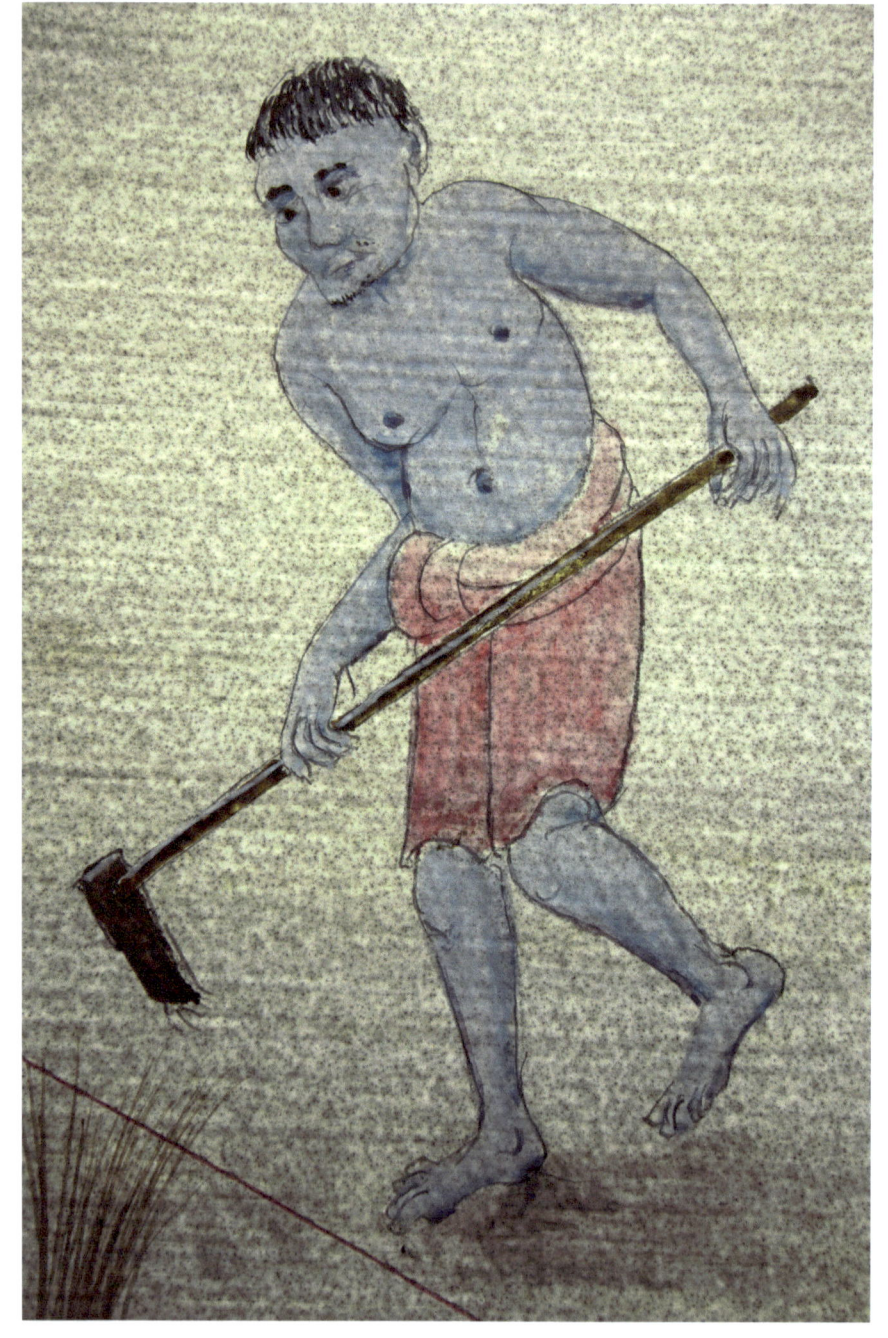

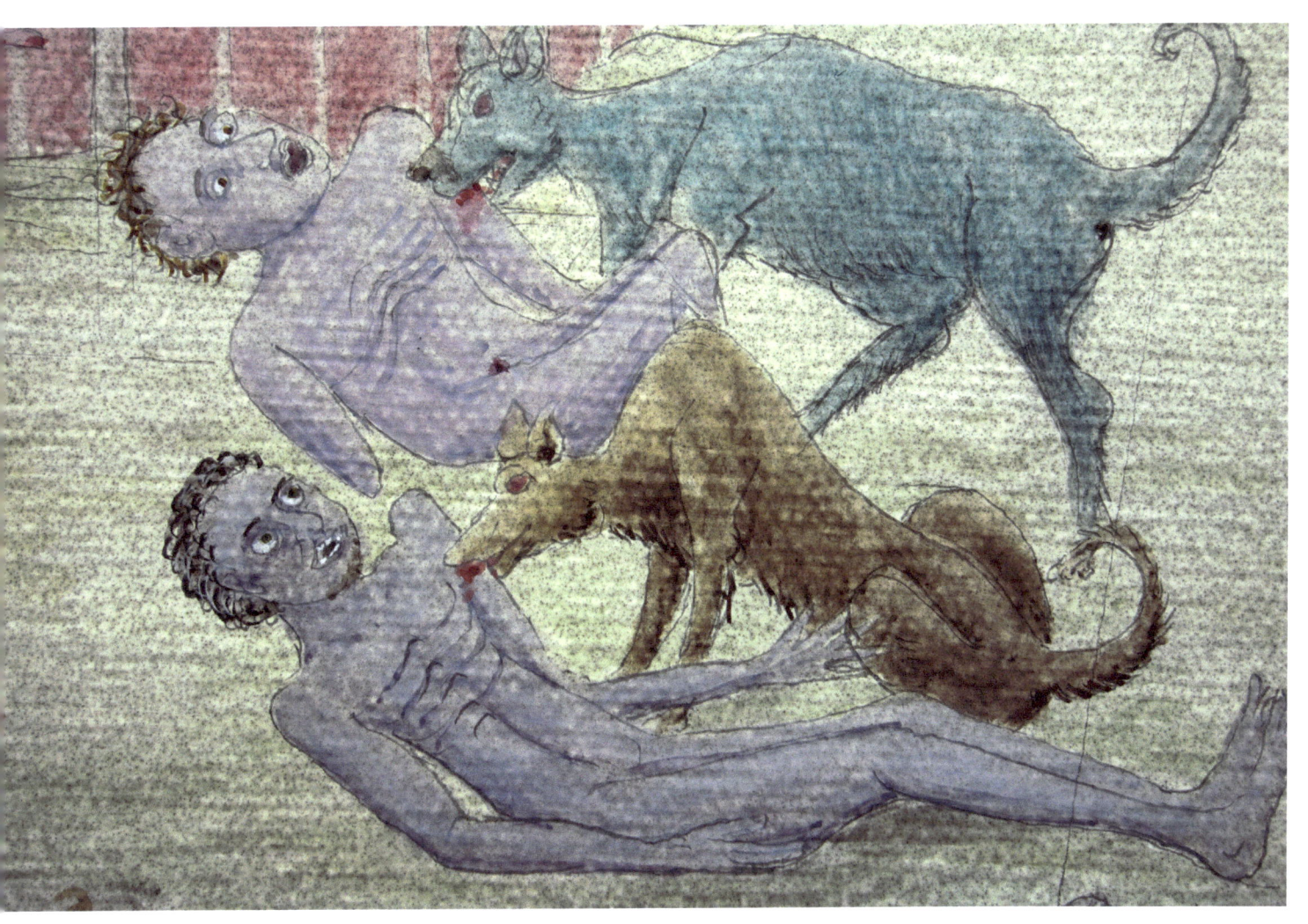

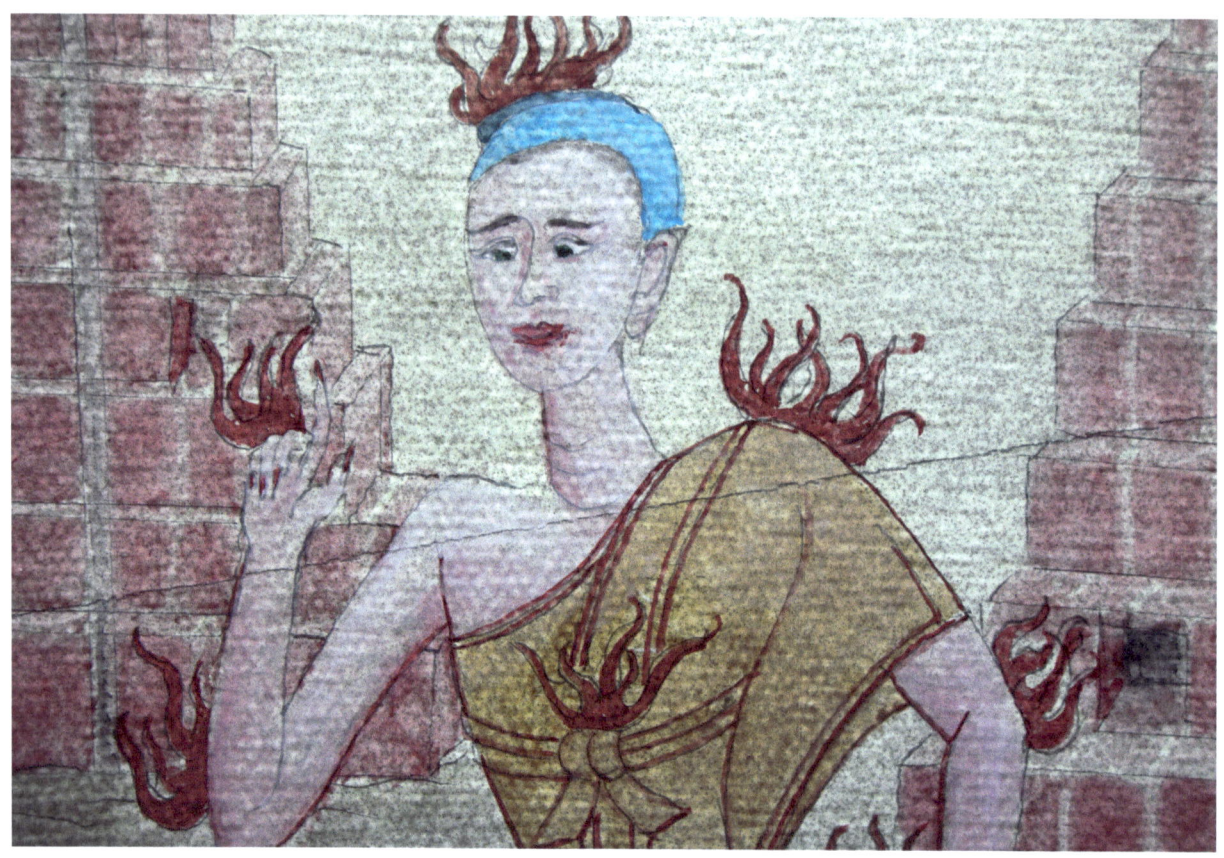

We found monuments heated past twenty torments.

 The flames stayed so intensely heated, all of their coverings uplifted, and dire laments tormented me.
"What are all those people having sex with?" I asked Her.

www.ingramcontent.com/pod-product-compliance
Lightning Source LLC
Chambersburg PA
CBHW041300180526
45172CB00003B/905